WHAT'S INSIDE?!?!

Take a journey throu~~gh~~ history and its

Learn about Edinburgh and Edinburgh Castle, Celtic and Gaelic Influence, Viking Rule, William Wallace, The Scottish Highlands and Caledonian Forrest, The Loch Ness Monster, Sheep and Scottish Highland Cows, Bagpipes, Kilts, Football and MORE!!!!

Every Kid History book is illustrated with a combination of characters and real-life pictures. Kid History is written in a way to help kids learn! Perfect for homeschooling or teaching someone about their heritage. Other titles include: "Let's Learn About"… Ireland, Canada, Australia, Spain, Mexico, United States of America, Egypt and more!

Hello and welcome to Kid Planet, Kid History!
My name is Reggie!

Today we will be learning about my home country.
It's a place filled with kilts, bagpipes and a MONSTER!!!

Today we are learning about…
SCOTLAND!

We begin our journey of Scotland in its capital, Edinburgh.

Edinburg is also home to the beautiful Edinburg Castle. The castle is a fortress that was built hundreds of years ago! The castle sits high a top a special place called, 'Castle Rock'!

The castle still stands today as a beautiful reminder of Scotland's history.

Did you know that Scotland is an island?!? It's located just off the coast of mainland Europe.

The first to arrive in what is now modern-day Scotland were a group called the Celts!

They were a peaceful group of traders but were also well-trained warriors! The Celtic culture helped form the foundation of what Scotland is today. Many families can trace their lineage back to the Celtic roots!

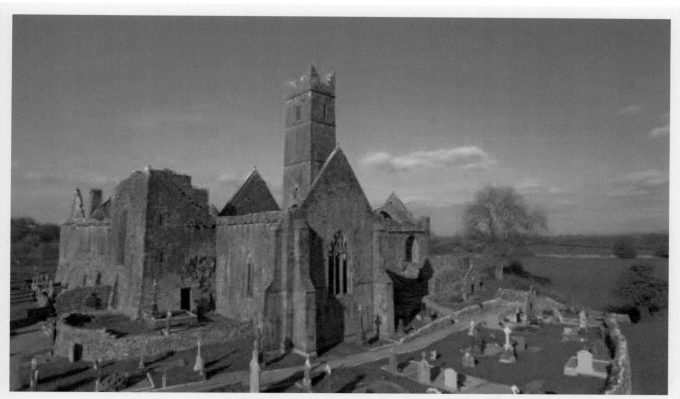

The Celts lived in Scotland and created settlements across the country. They were able to create roads, farms and communities. However, the Celtic settlers were no match for foreign invaders.

A group called the Vikings came from mainland Europe and invaded Scotland. The Vikings came from a different culture than the Celts and were not as peaceful as the natives. The Viking culture was one of warfare and conquering, and this was unfortunate for Scotland and the Celts.

It wasn't until 927 that the Vikings were finally defeated and left Scotland!

Once the Vikings left, the fighting didn't stop. One thing that we forgot to mention about Scotland is that it shares its island with the country of England.

For many years England and Scotland fought over land, religion and people. William Wallace is an iconic figure in Scottish history as he led battles against England in the 'First War of Scottish Independence'. The two countries continued to fight numerous other battles over the years.

Thankfully, England and Scotland have since settled their differences!

As a result of this new friendship, England passed the 'Acts of Union' which united Scotland, England and Wales to form Great Britain!

Let's Learn Some Scottish Cultural Facts...

The highlands are a historic region in Scotland. The highlands are known for their beauty and Scottish culture. They contain a place called the 'Caledonian Forest'. Some trees in this special forest have descendants that are over 9000 years old! The forest was also known to be one of the battle locations for the famous King Arthur!

Speaking of myths, did you know that Scotland is also home to ...

THE LOCH NESS MONSTER!

Loch or Lake Ness is located in the Scottish highlands that we learned about. The Loch Ness Monster or 'Nessie', as it is called is rumored to live in the loch. Nessie has been described as looking similar to a dinosaur with two humps, a large neck and swims!

Scotland isn't home to just monsters, it's also home to some wonderful cuddly animals! Scotland is a large provider of Wool. So don't be surprised if you visit Scotland and see lots of sheep!

Another amazing animal is called the Scottish highland cow! It is distinguished by two unique features. It has very large pointy horns and very long hair! Someone give that cow a haircut!

Scotland is world renowned for their bagpipe music!

Bagpipes are actually an instrument! They are part of the woodwind group. Bagpipes are made of an air sack with reeds attached. The bagpipe player blows air into the bag and then squeezes it to produce sound!

If you've never heard them before, imagine a noise that sounds like a goose playing an organ!

Wait.. Is that a dress? No! It's a kilt!

Scotland is famous for their kilts! The kilt originated in the 1500's in, you guessed it, the Scottish Highlands. It is a piece of clothing worn by men and boys. The kilt has remained a symbol of the Scottish culture for hundreds of years.

Many men of Scottish heritage still wear kilts to special occasions like weddings!

The Scots love their sports!

DID YOU KNOW?!?
Scotland was one of the first countries to organize sports.

The most famous sport in Scotland today is football or soccer.

Scotland loves their football!

LET'S REVIEW!

REVIEW

- CELTS
- VIKINGS
- WILLIAM WALLACE
- ACTS OF UNION
- HIGHLANDS

- LOCH MONSTER
- SHEEP & COWS
- BAGPIPES
- KILTS
- FOOTBALL

Until next time…

Grab your BAGPIPES…

say hello to THE LOCH NESS MONSTER…

and proudly wear your KILT!

Welcome to SCOTLAND!

Did you know?!?
Logan narrates
every
book on our
YouTube channel!

Search **"Logan Stover"** on YouTube
and **subscribe to Kid Planet!**

Please follow Kid Planet!

amazon.com/author/loganstover

facebook.com/kidplanetchildrensbooks

About the Kid Planet!

Logan Stover is a professional author and voice over actor.

He lives in Orange County, CA with his beautiful family.
Renowned for his unique "Shapeography" illustration techniques and his wonderful way of teaching children!

Printed in Great Britain
by Amazon

42803900R00017